Timepiece: Extending and Enhancing Learning Time

Edited by

Lorin W. Anderson

Herbert J. Walberg

National Association of Secondary School Principals

NASSP Staff

Timothy J. Dyer, Executive Director

James W. Keefe, Director of Research

Robert Mahaffey, Director of Publications and Marketing

Carol A. Bruce, Associate Director of Publications, Editor

Eugenia C. Potter, Technical Editor

Jody Guarino, Sr. Publications Specialist

ISBN 0–88210–280–X
Copyright 1993
National Association of Secondary School Principals
1904 Association Drive, Reston, Virginia 22091-1537
(703) 860-0200
PRINTED IN U.S.A.

Table of Contents

About the Authors

Lorin W. Anderson is Carolina research professor, University of South Carolina, Columbia.

Charles Ballinger is executive director, National Association for Year-Round Education, San Diego, Calif.

Fenwick W. English is professor of educational administration, University of Kentucky, Lexington.

D. Jean Clandinin is director, Centre for Research on Teacher Education and Development, Faculty of Education, University of Alberta, Canada

F. Michael Connelly is director, Joint Centre for Teacher Development, Ontario Institute for Studies in Education, Faculty of Education, University of Toronto, Canada

Laurence Steinberg is professor of psychology, Temple University, Philadelphia, Pa.

Herbert J. Walberg is research professor of education, University of Illinois at Chicago.

Foreword

Time is the most important commodity that we have. Its use is our most significant task, and acquired skill. Making time productive is one of the implicit goals of all attempts at school improvement and restructuring. The authors of this well-timed publication remind us of the many ways that time encapsulates our schools; they exhort us to find better ways to help students and teachers use it capably and wisely.

Most of us find time for what we really want to do. We make time for what we (and others) value as important. Our authors tell us that time for study, coordinated time cycles, academic learning time, personalized school schedules, year-round education, and cocurricular time are the elements that we should value in school time use. If school leaders, teachers, and students want schools to be more productive places, they will find the necessary time to use these timely elements.

Time is our scarcest educational resource. It is the most valuable thing we can spend. *Timepiece* tells us how we can do it.

James W. Keefe
NASSP Director of Research

Introduction and Overview

Herbert J. Walberg and Lorin W. Anderson

Learning, one of the most precious of all human activities, is central to educators' responsibilities. Time is a fundamental resource in human life and a key determinant of learning. Yet, American students spend less time learning than do students in other developed countries, and less time than they need to succeed in the coming information age. For these reasons, educators must think carefully about how educational time is and should be used.

That is the purpose of this book. The chapter authors—authorities on educational time use—have been asked to write succinctly and pointedly about how we can extend and enhance learning time within and outside school. The following brief summary of their views may be helpful in identifying the several themes of each chapter. The final chapter provides an analytic framework that presents and indexes the cross-cutting themes of the various chapters.

In "Productive Use of Time," Herbert Walberg argues that American students have considerable discretionary time that could be used for academic learning and other constructive pursuits. More than 100 studies demonstrate that the more students study, all other things being equal, the more they learn. Moreover, learning time can be extended and enhanced by using psychological principles.

In "Cycles, Rhythms, and the Meaning of School Time," Michael Connelly and Jean Clandinin suggest that—while schools are organized around logical, linear, and fixed units of time—parents, principals, teachers, and students experience time in cycles and rhythms. Annual cycles of holidays, and weekly cycles such as reviews on Mondays and tests on Fridays, create rhythms of experience that control the intensity of instruction.

In "What Time Tells Us," Lorin Anderson explains that we learn to tell time before we learn what time tells us. He differentiates several kinds of educational time: allocated and instructional time, time on task, and academic learning time. Comparisons among these types of time provide insights and useful information about classroom management, the quality of instruction, and student learning.

In "Changing the Cosmology of the School Schedule," Fenwick English attempts to engage readers in rethinking the social and cultural context of time. He begins with the factory model of school time that was developed during the industrial revolution. The balance of the chapter presents and discusses scheduling alternatives that are not based on the usual linear conceptions of school time.

In "Year-Round Education: It's Time," Charles Ballinger describes the assumptions underlying year-round schooling. These assumptions, he contends, correspond to the way humans learn: continuously. These assumptions challenge conventional thinking about the school year: when to start, when to stop, how long it should be, and when to take vacations. Since most states require students to be in school less than half the calendar year, it is possible to introduce great flexibility in organizing a year-round school year to meet individual needs and preferences.

In "The Use of Out-of-School Time," Laurence Steinberg shows that teenagers' lives outside school influence their learning and classroom engagement. Specifically, he examines the influences of activities like studying and reading that are widely thought to promote learning directly; part-time jobs, and cocurricular and other activities that may support learning directly or indirectly by promoting character or school connections; and still other activities such as television and "partying" with friends that are often thought to interfere with academic learning.

In the final chapter, we discuss several of the major issues of the book as revealed by a content analysis of the chapter themes. A table in this chapter presents a series of recommendations derived from the commonalities across the chapters.

Chapter 1

Productive Use of Time

Herbert J. Walberg

Time is one of the most important correlates of academic learning, and its linkage with learning is one of the most consistent findings in educational research. A 1980 review of 35 learning studies, for example, revealed that 86 percent showed a positive influence of time on learning. A 1992 review of more than 100 studies showed positive influences in 88 percent of the studies (Walberg and Fredrick, 1991). The average effect of increased learning time was comparable to the advantage of superior over mediocre instruction. The body of research literature suggests that large increases in productive learning time (other things being equal) can be expected to result in correspondingly large learning effects.

Still, Americans have yet to follow the obvious and long-standing implication of this research. In the widely-noted report of 1983, *A Nation at Risk*, the National Commission on Excellence in Education pointed out that a short school year and meager study time are among the major reasons for poor U.S. standings on international achievement comparisons.

Yet, the American school year generally remains about 180 days—the second shortest among 27 countries recently surveyed (Barrett, 1990). With a fourth and a third more annual school days, Germany's and Japan's students gain the equivalent of 15 and 16 years of American schooling by their twelfth year of school—not counting homework and other extramural study.

To attain challenging educational goals will require more and better learning time. For example, to achieve the national education goals posited by President Bush and the 50 state governors is a tall order. To make U.S. students first in the world in mathematics and science is an especially difficult challenge. Even to reach the middle of the group of industrialized countries will require considerably more productive time.

How Students Spend Time

During their first 18 years of life, American students spend only about 13 percent of their waking hours (and 8 percent of all hours) in school (Walberg, 1984). Six hours a day during a nine-month school year—1,080 hours—amounts to only about half of an adult work year (not counting holidays in either case). Even less time is actually spent learning because of absences, tardiness, inattentiveness, disruptions, noninstructional activities, and lessons that are too easy, too hard, or inappropriate in other ways.

What consumes the 87 percent of waking time spent outside school? On average, televisions are on continuously in more than 35 percent of American households during afternoon, dinner, and evening hours. American high school students report watching an average 28 hours of television per week during the school year—almost as much time as they spend in school; and they report an average of only 4 to 5 weekly hours of homework.

By comparison, Japanese students spend almost 50 percent more time in school and four to five times as much time on outside-school study. U.S. students spend substantially more time at work, sleeping, and socializing.

American adolescents study little, apparently because they dislike study. Except for work outside school, they prefer all other major activities to classwork, studying, and thinking. They strongly prefer being alone or with family and friends over time with classmates; and they rank time with strangers as only slightly less preferable than time with classmates (Csikszentmihalyi, 1982).

Time: Quantity vs. Quality

Karweit (1985) and others have argued that increasing school time would be wasteful, since some research suggests that students engage in academic activities only 38 percent of the school day. It would be possible, they suggest, to double academically-engaged time from 2.3 to 4.6 hours without exceeding the 6 or so hours of the ordinary school day.

Such an increase, however, is easier said than done. Educators cannot easily control absences, tardiness, and inattention; but they can reduce interruptions, distractions, and nonacademic activities. Good instruction—motivating and suitable—can also increase academically productive learning time.

In another sense, however, increasing the quality or suitability of instruction is particularly difficult in the U.S. (along with Australia, Canada, and Germany). Unlike most other industrialized (and developing) countries, the U.S. has no ministry of education that sets national goals (and detailed curriculum guidelines). Education is a state and local responsibility. As a result, much curriculum control in the U.S. is in the hands of state and local educational authorities, who differ from one another in their views and required curriculum offerings.

A student who moves from Maine to Illinois, for example, or even within a state, may encounter a very different curriculum and instructional program. For this reason, students who move risk a grade-level setback and learning deficit, especially if their families are lower in socioeconomic status. Since one of five American families moves each year, the problem is substantial.

The teacher's natural response to such students is to take class time to review previous work and to provide remediation for those incapable of grade-level work. The National Academy of Sciences identified this problem as a principal reason for U.S. students' poor standings in international comparisons of mathematics achievement.

If our nation responds successfully to the education goals of the president and governors, and to the congressional requirement for grade-level standards, this problem may be mitigated. If teachers could depend on what students had learned in the previous grade, they would be better able to differentiate instruction or to accelerate the pace of their teaching.

In any case, both the amount and quality of instruction are important and require improvement. There is no reason to think that American students can learn as much as students in other countries unless they have equal advantages in the amount and quality (or suitability) of their study.

The Psychology of Exceptional Learning

The study of eminent people reveals that their accomplishments are matters of opportunity and of continuous, concentrated effort over many years. When Isaac Newton, for example, was asked how he had managed to surpass the discoveries of his predecessors, he replied, "By always thinking about them." And the eminent mathematician, Friedrich Gauss, said, "If others would but reflect on mathematical truths as deeply and continuously as I have, they would make my discoveries."

Psychological studies of eminent painters, writers, musicians, and scholars of previous centuries reveal early, intense concentration on previous work in their fields, often to the near exclusion of other activities. Studies of prize-winning adolescents of our times also show intensive and extensive devotion to their chosen fields (Walberg, 1988).

The same fundamental thought processes appear to be required in both elementary and advanced study, as Simon (1981) and his colleagues have shown. The acquisition of information and the problem solving of beginners differ in degree rather than in kind from the mental activities of experts. The scarce resources are the amounts of time and concentration rather than the information available or the processing capacity of the mind—both of which, for practical purposes, seem unlimited.

Simon's work shows that the constraints on acquisition of knowledge and skills are the few items of information, perhaps two to seven, that can be held in short-term memory, and the time required—perhaps 5 to 10 seconds—to store an item in long-term memory. Experts differ from novices in science, chess, and other fields not only in having more information in permanent memory, but also by being able to retrieve and process it more efficiently.

Among experts, for example, items of information are more thoroughly indexed and thus can be rapidly brought to conscious memory. The items are elaborately associated or linked with one another. Two consequences of these associations—the ability to recover information by alternative links even when parts of the direct indexing are lost, and the capacity for trial-and-error searches—are the essential routines in problem solving, from the most elementary to the most advanced.

The greatest advantage of the expert is "chunking"—the representation of abstract groups of items as linked clusters that can be efficiently processed as an ensemble. Such chunks appear to underlie mental processes, from the childhood stages of cognitive development to scientific discoveries. Simon estimates that about 50 thousand chunks, about the same as the recognition vocabulary of college-educated readers, may be required for expert mastery of a special field.

The highest achievements in various disciplines, however, may require storage of roughly one million chunks. This amount may take even the talented about 70 hours of concentrated effort per week for a decade to acquire, although seven-to-nine-year-old exceptions, such as Wolfgang Mozart and Bobby Fisher, can be cited.

The prospect of such prodigious and sustained concentration might daunt novices. Yet, only a small fraction of the total is required for impressive achievement. Only an extra hour or two per day may enable children just beginning to attain results far beyond unpracticed adults in many fields such as music, chess, and foreign language.

Longer Study Time Isn't Stressful

Some educators fear that American children cannot sustain the longer hours of study necessary to achieve well by international standards. One source of anxiety about hard academic work stems from speculation that competitiveness, drive, and time urgency ("Type A behavior") cause coronary heart disease. The largest surveys, however, show that this pattern predicts no elevation in coronary disease. Rather, the psychological predictors of heart disease are depression and hostility.

What about suicides of hard-working Japanese students, who are well known for their prodigious amounts of study? For ages 10 to 19, Japanese suicide rates per 100,000 in 1984 were about half the U.S. rates, which have more than doubled since 1965—a period, according to U.S. education reform reports, of slackened educational standards and declining student effort.

Does effort cause unhappiness? Psychological research on optimal and exhilarating experiences shows that life's greatest pleasures include the development of skills and absorption in constructive activities. Research on adults, moreover, shows that such experiences are more often encountered in work than in leisure. High school students encounter them most often in opportunities that sufficiently challenge their skills—both in school and in outside pursuits (Csikszentmihalyi, 1982).

To be sure, students can work too hard. But average students seem far from that, if for no other reason than they watch nearly as much television as they spend in school. Television is sedentary and passive. It displaces homework, leisure reading, and active pursuits.

Although time and effort hardly seem causes of undue stress, too much external pressure can produce anxiety. If students feel driven by parents and teachers, if they fall far behind their peers and have little hope of catching up or blame themselves for failure, or if they lose a sense of control and autonomy, then they can become depressed, feel helpless, and suffer physical and emotional ills.

Encouragement, the setting of realistic goals, support and recognition for accomplishment, and learning for its own sake—these are always preferred over external coercion.

Productivity Theory Related to Time

In recent years, several breakthroughs have occurred in the analysis of large-scale educational surveys and in the syntheses of thousands of educational research results (see Walberg, 1984, for details). These surveys and syntheses show that nine major factors increase learning. Potent, consistent, and widely generalizable, these nine factors fall into the three groups shown in Table 1.

Table 1

Nine Educational Productivity Factors

A.   Student aptitude includes:

    1. Ability or prior achievement as measured by the usual standardized tests

    2. Development as indexed by chronological age or psychological stage

    3. Motivation or self-concept as indicated by personality tests or the student's willingness to persevere intensively on learning tasks.

B.   Instruction includes:

    4. The amount of time students spend in learning

    5. The quality or suitability of the instructional experience, including psychological and curricular aspects.

C.   The psychological environments bearing on academic learning include:

    6. The curriculum of the home or the academically stimulating environment provided by parents

    7. The classroom social group

    8. The peer group outside school

    9. The amount of leisure-time television viewing—the only negative factor.

Not only do these factors influence academic achievement but also affective and behavioral learning. Moreover, educators can affect them, especially the amount and quality of instruction.

Each of the first five factors—prior achievement, development, motivation, and the quantity and quality of instruction—seems necessary for learning in school; without at least a small amount of each, the student can learn little. Large amounts of instruction and high degrees of ability, for example, may count for little if students are unmotivated or if instruction is unsuitable.

If this theory is combined with insights from cognitive psychology (discussed above), it becomes apparent that time is a central and irreducible ingredient among the alterable factors in learning. Recall that the acquisition of an item of information requires an estimated 5 to 10 seconds; relating it "meaningfully" to assimilated chunks requires additional seconds; and problem solving or discovery by trial-and-error may take minutes, hours, days, or years.

But not all allocated time in school and outside study is employed for the fundamental processes of learning and discovery. Quality of instruction, for example, can be understood to include providing optimal cues, correctives, and reinforcement to ensure successful engaged time. Diagnosis and tutoring can help ensure that instruction is suitable to the individual student. Inspired teaching can enhance motivation to keep students persevering. Quality of instruction, then, may be thought of as efficient enhancement of allocated and engaged learning time.

Similarly, the four psychological environments shown in Table 1 can enlarge and enhance the productive use of learning time. Good classroom morale may reflect the match of the lesson to student aptitude, the socially stimulating properties of the academic group, or, in general, the degree to which students are concentrating on learning rather than diverting their energies because of unconstructive social climates.

Peer groups outside school and stimulating home environments can help by enlarging learning time and enhancing its efficiency. Students can learn important material directly in the home and in peer-group environments, as well as become better able to learn effectively in school. Unfortunately, television watching can displace homework, leisure reading, and other stimulating activities; it may also dull the student's keenness for academic work. Some of the 28 hours a week that high school students spend viewing television might usefully be added to the mere 4 or 5 weekly hours of homework they report.

Psychological Principles of Time Use

Four areas of psychological research on the productive use of time suggest principles that may be applied to curriculum and instruction. They are discussed briefly in this section.

■ *Spacing of Practice.* One of the most dependable findings from psychology holds up in classroom research: that "spaced" practice over several lessons or study periods is superior to equal amounts of time spent in "massed" practice (concentrated, possibly in one session). Indeed, two spaced presentations, or practice sessions, are about twice as effective as two successive (massed) presentations of the same length.

Moreover, achievement following an extended massed presentation is often only slightly higher than achievement following a single shorter presentation. Massed presentations may, of course, be unnecessarily repetitive; and one reason for spacing's efficiency is that students may be more interested in material the second time after some delay (Dempster, 1987).

There is some validity, however, to student intuitions that "cramming" can be time-efficient for scoring well on tests, even though material may be soon forgotten. In this regard, frequent quizzes and oral questions may be effective in countering what is efficient for short-term memory but inefficient for long-term retention. Making the subject matter intrinsically interesting, however, is even more attractive.

■ *Direct Acquisition.* Contrary to what many psychologists had earlier believed, elaborated learning ("meaningful" association of new material with old) is not necessarily superior to spending time on direct acquisition—that is, memorization or concentration on the main points to be retained. Word knowledge, for example, can be increased at least as much by a definition-only approach as it can by gaining understanding from context. Students have also attained more from reading summaries than unabridged texts, even when main points in the unabridged text were underlined (Dempster, 1987).

Obviously, if contextual and peripheral material is considered part of the required subject matter content, then studying it is time well spent. If not, it is more time efficient to make goals explicit and for students to concentrate on the main points.

Which is more important: the amount of information or its connectedness? Breadth or depth? Reasonable people may differ on the amounts of time devoted to each in various subjects, but all need to recognize that time on earth and time for learning are limited.

■ *Non-Diminishing Returns.* Athletic training often shows diminishing returns; that is, increasing the number of hours of swimming or running each week, for example, can lead to ever smaller gains (and even losses at the extremes). Diminishing gains, however, have not been consistently observed in cognitive learning and academic achievement. Simon's (1981) assertion that, for practical purposes, both the extent of knowledge and the processing capacity of the mind are infinite may explain why memory and related skills can apparently increase constantly with additional time, at least within the normal ranges that have been studied.

■ *The Matthew Effect.* Students who are behind at the beginning of schooling, or slow to start, often learn at a slower rate; those who start ahead gain at a faster rate. This pattern results in what has been called the "Matthew Effect" (Walberg 1984)— the academically rich getting richer, while the poor get poorer, as exemplified in the "Book of Matthew" in the Bible. Although improved instructional programs may benefit all students, they may confer greater advantages on those who are initially advantaged. For this reason, the first six years of life and the "curriculum of the home" are decisive influences on academic achievement.

Productive Time

Increasing the amount of time available for learning and making it more productive are keys to improved learning. Educators, parents, and policymakers may consider and carry out a number of effective policies toward this end, such as pre-school, half-day and full-day kindergarten, active stimulation of children by parents at home, and constructive television watching of "Electric Company," "NOVA," and similar programs.

Educators may also consider instructional methods and motivational techniques to increase instructional time. Possibilities include employing more homework with feedback, extended-day school with academic encouragement and assistance, and summer school for children who fall behind. Districts and states would be wise to contemplate increasing the number of days in the regular school year and the number of hours in the school day.

But increases in "productive time," that fraction of lesson and study time during which students actually learn, are also in order. Ordinarily, only a fraction of instructional time is productive, since conventional, whole-group instruction cannot accommodate the vast differences in student learning rates and prior knowledge; and since students with weak study skills can engage in study without really learning. To accommodate such differences, and to reduce the "Matthew effects," lessons can and should be made more suitable to individual learners, and students should be taught to concentrate more fully on what they individually require.

References

Barrett, M. J. "The Case for More School Days." *The Atlantic Monthly*, November 1990, pp. 78–106.

Csikszentmihalyi, M. "Toward a Psychology of Optimal Experience." *Review of Personality and Social Psychology* 45(1982): 317–18.

Dempster, F.N. "Time and the Production of Classroom Learning: Discerning Implications from Basic Research." *Educational Psychologist* 1(1987): 1–21.

Karweit, N. "Should We Lengthen the School Term?" *Educational Researcher* 6 (1985): 9–15.

Simon, H. A. *Sciences of the Artificial.* Cambridge, Mass.: MIT Press, 1981.

Walberg, H. J. "Improving the Productivity of America's Schools." *Educational Leadership* 8(1984): 19–27.

———. "Creativity as Learning." In *The Nature of Creativity,* edited by R. Sternberg. New York: Cambridge University Press, 1988.

Wallberg, H. J., and Fredrick, W. C. *Extending Learning Time.* Washington, D.C.: U.S. Department of Education, 1991.

Cycles, Rhythms, and the Meaning of School Time

F. Michael Connelly and D. Jean Clandinin

An important idea stands behind this book. It is that time must be brought out of the taken-for-granted shadows and made a deliberate part of school planning. A breakthrough on time came when researchers demonstrated that, in general, the more time is spent learning, the more is learned. Nobody was surprised by this finding. It was so obvious that some scholars called the observation "trivially true." But the finding wasn't trivial except in a strictly logical sense.

Together, the authors of this chapter have spent roughly 50 years teaching and being concerned about curriculum and instruction in schools and universities. As a result of these experiences, we have come to believe that what is called "curriculum planning" could as easily be called "organizing time." High-minded arguments about the relative importance of particular content topics are often best understood in terms of what to do with limited time. Time, not content, is often the main concern. Accordingly, the allocation and use of time is an important, intuitively obvious, basis for thinking about curriculum and teaching.

However, this insight runs counter to another intuition: that learning depends on the intensity of the learning experience. Everyone knows that they learn best at certain times of the day, week, and year. People have learning highs and learning lows. Teachers know that gripping events such as a football game, the World Series, or an evening soap opera make a difference to the equation, "more time equals more learning."

The personal experience of school time makes a great deal of difference to the learning of curriculum content. Furthermore, the personal experience of school time depends on the temporal structure of schools. Few institutions are as temporally complicated and run by the clock as schools. This temporal structure affects the intensity with which students, teachers, administrators, and others personally experience school time. We believe that the intensity with which time is experienced is at least as important as the amount of time that is experienced.

One of the profound difficulties in school planning is the discrepancy between the mathematical, linear *logic* of time, and the cyclic, rhythmic *experience* of time. This discrepancy is something like a conundrum in the theoretical physics of optics: Sometimes light phenomena are best understood as waves, sometimes as particles. The dilemma of sorting out the "wave theory" of light from the "particle theory" of light has productively preoccupied physicists. School planning and organization might also be more productive if educators were able to confront apparent conflicts between linear/mathematical/logical time and cyclic/rhythmic/experiential time.

We have all heard the phrase "time's arrow," used to convey a sense of temporal inevitability from past through present, and into the future. Clock time has quantified "time's arrow," and time is everywhere counted out in unvarying units. These units have become so important to modern life that they are equivalent to a universal standard like radioactive isotope decay. Schools are organized and run according to this mathematical/physical standard. A school year is defined by a specific number of days; a school day is defined by a specific number of minutes. School budgets are connected to the number of days a school is open, the number of children-days of attendance, and so forth.

But the clock face, at least the old-style analogical one, tells a different story. It has a round face; time goes around and measures out temporal cycles of seconds, minutes, and hours. Time, according to the analogical clock, goes around, not forward, as does "time's arrow." This cyclical quality is not mere accident or convention; it is directly connected to the nature of the universe with cycles of light and darkness, sleep and wakefulness, growth and decay. Life as a whole is experienced as a life cycle. Cyclic temporal structures are experienced rhythmically so that it is common to refer to "the rhythm of life," "the rhythm of the seasons," and the "rhythm of the school."

Temporal cycles make a difference in the way time is experienced. Just as the experience of time throughout a day differs for parts of the day, the experience of life differs for parts of a life cycle. Time is experienced differently as a child than as a parent, or as a senior citizen. Yet, in the linear sense of time, the moments are of equal mathematical length. From commonplace observation, it is easy to see that both the amount and the experience of time make a difference in learning. The experience of time, in turn, depends on the part of the cycle one is experiencing.

School Cycles

Let us look at schools from the point of view of temporal cycles. With a little imagination one can visualize a series of cycles within cycles, and cycles interacting with cycles. Some of the cycles are marked out with a clock face, and some look like a calendar, but they all go around. It is a little like one of those surrealistic mechanical sculptures where everything is connected and turning. While this temporal image of schooling may be slightly dizzying, it does make sense, as do the sculptures, when closely examined.

School cycles have several characteristics that are important to learning. First, cycles are relatively inflexible, a little like the gears in an old-style mechanical clock. A principal, teacher, student, or parent tampers with one of the spinning cogs at great risk (e.g., a student coming to class late, a teacher deciding to start a class 10 minutes early, a principal starting the school year one day late, a parent requesting an appointment in the middle of a lesson). These temporal boundary lines are quite fixed, and constitute a very large part of the school's supposed moral and ethical structure. Teachers who don't start their classes on time, or students who come late are judged to be not only in violation of school rules but morally wanting: lazy, inconsiderate of others, selfish, incompetent.

Second, cycles are not mere circles of time; they have a particular temporal structure. They have a beginning, middle, and end, like the life cycles of birth, life, and death.

Consider, for instance, the daily school cycles of activities. At the beginning of the day, students store materials in lockers, fetch other materials, and greet friends as they make their way to class. Students experience these few minutes before school very differently than the same amount of time as they bolt from school at the end of the day. Both of these experiences differ from class and lesson time that makes up the middle of the daily cycle. Within a lesson, the same qualitative differences in the experience of time occur during lesson start-up, execution, and completion.

Third, there are many overlapping cycles of activities that each person experiences simultaneously. A lesson cycle is part of a daily cycle, which is part of a weekly cycle, which may be a part of a semester cycle, which is part of an annual cycle.

Fourth, every teacher knows that the harmonious interaction of these cycles makes a difference to teaching and learning; e.g., the same lesson taught in the morning may be experienced differently in the afternoon if the school's sports cycle affects that lesson. Thus, how a unit of instructional time is experienced depends not only on the duration of instruction, but also on its place in the structure of cycles and how its cycle interacts with other cycles.

Two teachers in a school where we worked for a number of years had vastly different experiences of holiday and lesson cycles. One teacher built her lessons around the holidays and loved the momentum given to instruction by impending celebrations. The other teacher virtually gave up teaching as holidays approached and students became too rambunctious to follow his lesson plan.

Fifth, cycles have fixed boundary lines that rigidly structure a school's social life. The forcing of activities into cyclic patterns creates school routines and rituals that influence the intensity and meaning of instruction. These routines and rituals are so pronounced and identified with specific cycles that school people can tell school time without the aid of a clock, simply by noting activities.

Consider, for example, the routines and rituals of opening and closing the school, of opening and closing a reading lesson, of school assemblies, of cyclic examination cycles, and so on. As each cycle unfolds with its associated routines and rituals, the social behavior of teachers, students, and others is prescribed. Cycles and their associated calendars, routines, and rituals create a schedule in which virtually every moment of time is accounted for in some way.

Zerubavel (1979), in his study of hospital time, pointed out that temporal regularity, when it reaches high levels as it does in schools, is an enemy of spontaneity. Similarly, teachers who plan for creativity and spontaneity in their lesson time stand in opposition to the overall experience of school time, which is one of cyclic regularity and associated routines and rituals. Spontaneity is not simply under instructional control, as many who promote its value would have us believe. It is, to a large extent, subject to the ongoing experience of school time, which, unfortunately, does not favor spontaneity.

Finally, the cyclical structure is so much a part of school life that people tend to feel they have little control over time. People seem to dance like marionettes on the cog wheels of the clock. Although life as a whole is experienced cyclically, school cycles are almost entirely without natural reference. Life cycles appear to be given, normal, and natural, but school cycles are artificial. They are "made up."

People often argue that the September-to-June yearly school cycle has a natural connection with agricultural cycles. For many in North America, however, this natural connection vanished as society became urbanized. The discussion about the possibility of changing the school year often sounds like a religious discussion, as if something fundamentally natural was being violated. In fact, school cycles are created by humans, and may easily be remade.

Proponents of modifying the school year are on strong grounds when they argue that changing the cycle will change students', teachers', principals', and parents' experience of the school year, and will thereby contribute differently to learning. At the same time, the rigid social structure associated with the annual cycle makes opposition to a changed school year understandable. Parents have cycles of holidays and work connected to the annual school cycle. Teachers' salaries and benefits are closely tied to it. Changing the school cycle can disrupt these and other associated cycles.

Examples of School Cycles

We have identified at least 10 school cycles according to their temporal duration: annual, holiday, monthly, weekly, six-day, duty, day, teacher, report, and within-class cycles. These cycles not only vary in duration, but also according to sequence, temporal location, and rate of occurrence. Space does not allow us to analyze each of these cycles in depth, but we will illustrate the relationships between a lesson cycle, a within-class cycle, and a report cycle.

A lesson is something like a story, in that it has a beginning, middle, and end, directly linked to the temporal structure of a within-class cycle. The structure is more clearly seen in the secondary school than in the elementary school. The within-class lesson cycle of secondary schools is comparatively rigid. Bells ring and classes change; activities begin, are worked through, and conclude. However, the within-class cycles and the lesson cycles often do not coincide. Lessons frequently extend over a series of class periods.

The way these two cycles interact clearly influences teaching and learning. Students, for example, may be in the middle of a lesson when the class bell signals the end of a period. When students return the next day, the intellectual intensity of the lesson may have dissipated and be further affected as class start-up routines take place. By the time students "get up to speed," the class period may be over.

A lesson that might have been completed uninterrupted, with certain learning outcomes in a certain amount of time, is modified by the temporal demands of the within-class cycle. Thoughtful teachers understand these interactions as they plan lessons in terms of other cycles (e.g., the sports cycle).

In contrast to the secondary school, the structure of lessons in an elementary school is less rigid and more blurred, but even here most activities have the basic structure of a beginning, middle, and end. It is increasingly easy, however, for teachers and students to blur the cyclic boundaries and introduce more personalized responses within the units of time.

In restructuring schools, especially secondary schools, we believe that one of the potentially most effective means of changing and improving students' experience of school is to make the cyclic lesson structure less rigid and more responsive. Secondary school teachers often find it difficult to comprehend flexible planning because they are so heavily geared to subject matter organized in terms of annual, semester, and daily lesson cycles.

School reporting schedules are worked out within broad school board parameters. In secondary schools particularly, students and teachers know precisely where they are in the reporting cycles during which students are tested, grades computed, report cards written and transmitted to parents, parents interviewed, and a new cycle begun. What is learned is heavily influenced by the particular part of the reporting cycle in which learning occurs. Time is experienced differently following testing and reporting than it is during the period before testing and reporting. Learning varies accordingly.

As local boards and state or provincial governments add testing programs, these programs will interact more or less harmoniously with the ongoing report cycles already in place. For many students in secondary schools, these newly imposed cycles may disrupt the rhythm of reporting cycles, and students may come to feel as if they are in a continuous testing environment. The negative consequences for learning are obvious.

The point here is that the report cycle has its own rhythm and meaning for teachers and students alike. The disruption of that rhythm makes it increasingly difficult to experience normal learning. There is less learning time because of testing, and the rhythm of the reporting period—its sense of a beginning, middle, and end—is disrupted.

Cycles, the Temporal Order, and the Experience of Time

Two stories of how these cycles create temporal order in schools will illustrate the meaning of "school time." The first story speaks of what some teachers and students characterize as a "treadmill of activities." Administrators in schools spend countless hours each year scheduling the many school cycles. By the beginning of school in the fall, cycles are in place, and teachers and students begin to develop a rhythm of the cycles.

Teachers tell us that they actually create another cycle (Craig, 1992). They speak of early fall days spent planning cocurricular events such as the fall open house, the sports program, December celebrations, school dances, and so on.

Even as they create these cocurricular events, they know that they are actually establishing a cycle through which they will inevitably be drawn. They know, for example, that as the basketball season winds down to a climax of tournaments and play-offs, track and field is already beginning its process of training and team selection. They know that, as the choir assembles in the fall, it will move through practices and performances throughout the year.

Fortunately, these cycles interact more or less harmoniously for students and teachers. When curriculum and cocurriculum demands are more in conflict than in harmony, teachers and students talk about being "scattered," "unfocused," "too busy," and "fragmented."

Stevenson (1990) reflected on a move from a grade 7–12 school, in which she was an effective teacher, to a grade 7–9 arrangement. She wrote:

Within hours after entering my new assignment, I was totally distraught over my inability to be the kind of teacher that I knew how to be. Why did I have the feeling that I was out of step from the very beginning? After all, wasn't teaching junior high students the same anywhere? Why could I not envision the year to come in terms of units and break this down into a logical sequence of planning? With my timetable in front of me, why could I not begin to organize my days according to where I had to be and when I had to be there?

If this is so for a teacher, imagine how students' experiences are changed as they move from teacher to teacher with different lesson and class cycles, and as they move through the grades and divisions over the years.

These illustrations highlight the profoundly different ways in which time is experienced in schools. Thinking of time as linear and mathematical leads to the important maxim, "time is learning." But our reflections on the cyclical structure of school time and its rhythmic experience enable us to see that the maxim can easily be swamped in a maelstrom of teacher/student experiences.

As the second illustration shows, teachers can be thrown into unproductive rhythms by changes in cycles. To think that more time on task will automatically lead to more learning is to ignore the fact that both teachers and students experience units of time differently, depending on their temporal cycles and their personal interactions. The intensity of teaching and of learning make the difference.

References

Craig, C. "Developing Personal Practical Knowledge of Teaching: The Beginning Teachers' Experience." Doctoral dissertation, University of Alberta, 1992.

Stevenson, S. "Rhythms and Cycles: I Got Those Low Down, No Good, Transfer Blues." Unpublished paper, University of Calgary, 1990.

Zerubavel, M. *Patterns of Time in Hospital Life: A Sociological Perspective.* Chicago: The University of Chicago Press, 1979.

What Time Tells Us

Lorin W. Anderson

We grow up learning to tell time. For many of us, the ability to tell time, along with the ability to read our first words, write our names, and count to 10 or 20, represent our first recognized academic accomplishments. In fact, telling time allows us to develop socially valued traits such as promptness (being on time) and perseverance (working continuously until finished or time to quit).

As we grow older, we begin to realize that time tells us many things. Time tells us that we are not as young as we once were. When we reach middle age, for example, we are unable to "party 'til we drop" and still meet the demands of the next day. We begin to regret time lost or wasted, and we look for ways to save time.

During the 1970s, educational researchers developed an interest in telling time (Denham and Lieberman, 1980; Anderson, 1984; Fisher and Berliner, 1985). They learned to tell how much time was given to the study of various subjects. They counted the time that was lost because of administrative interruptions and poorly planned or delivered lessons. They studied how much time students spent daydreaming or otherwise uninvolved in learning. Finally, they learned to estimate the portion of classroom time in which students were successful in attempts to learn.

As might be expected, critics of this research wondered exactly what this study of time told them. Gage (1978), for example, contended that time was a "psychologically empty quantitative concept" (p. 75). Stallings (1980) and Frymier (1981) argued that there was a need to move "beyond time" if teaching and learning were to be understood and improved. Finally, Phillips (1985) suggested that most of the things time told him were "patently obvious" and "trivially true" (p. 311).

Unfortunately, either the critics were not listening carefully to what time had to say, or the researchers did not clearly communicate time's message. For whatever reason, educator's interest in time declined during the 1980s. Entering the '90s, we must reflect once again on that decade of unparalleled research on the allocation and use of school time and see whether the message of the previous decade can be salvaged.

Telling Time

In their attempts to study time, educational researchers have identified four primary temporal categories: allocated time, instructional time, time-on-task, and academic learning time. A description of each type follows. A summary of the relationships among the various categories of time is displayed in Figure 1.

Allocated time can be defined as the amount of time during which children attend school, or the amount of time that children, while in school, are scheduled to study particular subjects. Allocated time can be expressed in terms of years, days, or hours.

Children typically are required to attend school a minimum of 10 years (excluding kindergarten). Each year, they are expected to spend at least 180 days in school, with each school day lasting a minimum of six hours. Thus, on the average, somewhat more than 10,000 hours are allocated for each child to compulsory schooling.

If we consider a single subject (e.g., science), a similar analysis is possible. In this country, we typically require high school students to complete two years of science. These students attend school approximately 180 days per year. Each day, they attend 40 to 60 minutes of science instruction. Thus, we allocate a minimum of 240 hours to the study and learning of high school science. (In light of this number, it is instructive to ask ourselves how much science high school students can be expected to learn in the equivalent of 30 8-hour days.)

Figure 1

Relationships among Allocated Time, Instructional Time, Time-on-Task, and Academic Learning Time

Allocated Time		100 percent
Instructional Time		83.3 percent
Time-on-Task		62.5 percent
Academic Learning Time		41.7 percent
		0 percent

Instructional Time

Instructional time is the amount of allocated time in school during which instruction is provided to students. In order to understand instructional time, it is useful to consider the time when students are in school but are not receiving instruction. All students eat lunch. Elementary school students have recess. High school students may have study hall (they may or may not study). These time periods, although important, decrease the amount of school time spent on instruction.

Similarly, not all class time is spent on instruction. Classes may be interrupted by intercom announcements, attendance checks, tardy students, the distribution and collection of papers, or a dispute between two students. In science classes, time may be used to set up laboratory equipment or to clean up once the laboratory lesson is completed. Time may be needed to move students from one place to another.

All these examples are instances of noninstructional allocated time. A great deal of research indicates that approximately one-sixth of the allocated classroom time is spend on noninstructional activities, with a range from 7 to 24 percent (Burns, 1984; Anderson, Ryan, and Shapiro, 1989). About five-sixths of the time, then, is spent on instruction.

Time-on-Task (TOT)

Time-on-task is the amount of instructional time during which a student or a group of students is attending to the appropriate task, or is actually engaged in learning. Because of the latter, time-on-task is also referred to as engaged time.

Few, if any, students are attentive or engaged every minute in their classrooms. They fidget, they daydream, and they are distracted by other students and events inside or outside the classroom. Sometimes, they are simply bored.

Several studies suggest that students can be expected to be on-task approximately three-fourths of the time they are receiving classroom instruction, with a range from 38 percent (Smyth, 1985) to 96 percent (Anderson, Ryan, and Shapiro, 1989).

Academic Learning Time (ALT)

Academic learning time is that portion of classroom time during which students are working on important objectives or tasks (typically those included on end-of-term or end-of-year tests); actually on-task or engaged in learning related to those objectives; *and* successful in their learning endeavors. The second part of this definition is identical to the one for time-on-task given earlier. In addition to being on-task, however, academic learning time requires that students must be working on an important objective or task and be successful in their attempts to accomplish that objective or task.

As might be expected, the amount of academic learning time is typically less than the amount of time-on-task. In fact, the few estimates we have of academic learning time suggest that it amounts to about two-thirds of the amount of the time students spend on-task (Fisher et al., 1978). Depending on the quality of instruction, academic learning time may range from 0 to almost one 100 percent.

What Time Tells Us

Despite views to the contrary, understanding the meaning of time is not a simple matter. Objectively, we know that an hour is an hour. This objective view of time may lead us to believe that more is better; that more time spent on learning will result in greater learning. Subjectively, however, time means different things to different people at different times.

When we are in love, time seems to fly. An hour with that special person can seem like a minute. When we are waiting for a special day (e.g., wedding, birthday), time can drag. An hour may seem like a year.

A critical difference exists between the *measure* of time (how we tell time), and the *meaning* of time, (what time tells us). The implications of our understanding of time are discussed in this section.

Allocated time tells us about our educational values; what we think is important for students to study and learn in our schools. From the way in which we currently allocate time in elementary school classrooms, we know that reading and language arts are more important than all other subject areas (Burns, 1984). The time allocated to reading and language arts is almost equal to the total amount of time allocated to mathematics, science, social studies, music, art, and physical education combined. Literacy, then, is a value basic to our elementary education system (which makes the current statistics on illiteracy in the United States even more depressing).

In secondary schools, English again is paramount. To graduate from high school, students in many states need at least one more Carnegie Unit of English than any other subject. Competency in mathematics, science, and social studies is somewhat less emphasized. Competency in music, art, and physical education is even less important.

Within specific subject areas, the allocation of time once again tells us about our values. Teaching students to work with other students and to engage in discussion are valued as less important than teaching them understanding (Burns, 1984). Reviewing previously taught material is considered more important than introducing new material (Anderson, Ryan, and Shapiro, 1989).

Instructional time, by itself, tells us very little. When it is compared with allocated time, however, it means a great deal. The discrepancy between allocated and instructional time tells us about the quality of classroom management. The greater the discrepancy, the poorer the classroom management. It is not unusual for 20 percent of the time allocated to subject area study to be lost on noninstructional activities (e.g., announcements, interruptions, dead time, and discipline). Teachers who spend substantially less than this proportion of allocated time are better classroom managers; those who spend substantially more are poorer managers.

Like instructional time, time-on-task by itself tells us little. No students can be on task all the time, so it makes no sense to suggest that having all students on task all the time is a desirable goal. Helpful information for educators and researchers comes from comparing instructional time with time-on-task. Stated simply, the greater the amount of instructional time that students are on task, the higher the quality of instruction.

As a point of reference, it is not unusual for students to be off task for about one-fourth of the time that instruction is occurring. Thus, teachers who can engage their students in learning more than three-fourths of the instructional time likely are providing higher quality instruction. Those who engage their students in learning for less than three-quarters of the time are providing instruction of lower quality.

Finally, academic learning time derives its real meaning from a comparison with time-on-task. The discrepancy between academic learning time and time-on-task provides a reasonable estimate of the quality of student learning. The closer that the amount of academic learning time approximates the amount of time-on-task, the more likely it is that students are learning what is appropriate and expected. When the amount of academic learning time is substantially less than the amount of time-on-task, students likely are not learning what is expected.

Improving Education Through Our Understanding of Time

In view of the previous discussion, it is instructive to examine the typical loss of time for a typical student in a typical classroom. Suppose, for example, that a high school allocated 60 minutes per day to the study of science. According to the available research, approximately 50 of these minutes would be spent on instruction.

During approximately 38 of the minutes, students would be on task or engaged in learning. For approximately 25 of these minutes, students would be successful in their attempts to learn something important enough to be assessed and evaluated. Stated somewhat differently, the typical student in our high schools today is actually learning what is expected less than half the time that he or she is in the classroom.

To increase the effectiveness and efficiency of student learning, then, we educators must allocate time to those things we believe are most important for students to learn; devote as much allocated time to instruction as is possible; find ways to engage students in learning during the time instruction is provided; and, help students achieve success on those learning tasks that we believe to be important.[1] Recommendations concerning each of these issues are presented and discussed in the next sections.

Allocated Time and Educational Values

The ways that we allocate time are critical to the quality of education, because students spend only so much time in schools and in classrooms. Currently, a great deal of time in many high school classrooms is allocated to the memorization of facts and the rote application of rules.

Substantially less time is spent developing the concepts that students must understand. Similarly, much time is spent by students repeating almost verbatim what their teacher says or what is found in textbooks. Far less time is spent helping students express and defend their opinions about the subject matter. As a consequence, students come to believe that subject matter consists of "truths," rather than theories, hypotheses, and viewpoints. Educators must ask whether this, in fact, is the kind of education we value.

Improving Classroom Management

During the past two decades, much has been learned about maximizing the amount of allocated time that is actually spent on instruction. For example, intrusions into the classroom should be minimized (i.e., announcements over the intercom, visits from administrators, arrival of late students). In addition, rules for appropriate classroom behavior should be established and communicated to the students. Whenever possible, these rules should permit and encourage students to monitor their own behavior (rather than have their behavior monitored only by the teacher).

Finally, routines for conducting typical classroom business should be established

---

1. This analysis focuses exclusively on the allocation and productive use of time in schools. School time represents only a small fraction of the total time available for instruction and learning (Chapter 1). Thus, as Steinberg mentions in Chapter 6, more productive use of out-of-school time is also important.

and followed consistently (e.g., entering and leaving the classroom, passing out papers and collecting assignments, making announcements and taking attendance). With attendance, for example, it is usually more efficient to identify who is absent, not who is present.

Improving Classroom Instruction

Classroom instruction is of the highest quality when time-on-task or engaged time is maximized. Twenty years of research have shown us a great deal about maximizing time-on-task. In general, students are more likely to spend more time on-task when:
1. They understand clearly what is expected of them; specifically, they know what they are to learn, how they are to learn it, how they are to demonstrate that they have learned, and how the quality of their learning is to be evaluated.
2. They interact with, or have their work monitored by, their teachers or peers; that is, contact time and concern for the quality of student learning tend to increase time-on-task.
3. They are placed in situations or settings with "holding power;" that is, settings that focus students' attention on the task at hand, insulate them from external distractions, and enable them to monitor their own successes and make corrections when needed.
4. They know they are expected to learn and are reinforced for exerting the necessary effort (e.g., praise or incentives).
5. They are given assignments that are interesting, challenging, or both.

Enhancing Student Learning

In our analysis of time, the key to enhancing student learning is to increase student academic learning time. Several recommendations can be offered in this regard.

First, the majority of objectives and tasks assigned to students should be important enough to be included on tests and other assessments used to evaluate their learning.

Second, the objectives and assignments given to students should be sequenced, whenever possible, to help them move from their current knowledge and skills to the types and levels they will need in the future.

Third, effort should be made to ensure high degrees of student success early in the sequence.

Fourth, educators must know when students feel they are successful. Arbitrary and relative grading standards do not necessarily equate with success in the minds of students. Similarly, students who answer every question correctly do not necessarily perceive themselves as successful.

Finally, teachers must help students overcome their initial errors and misunderstandings by providing feedback and correction. Students must be taught that errors and misunderstandings must be overcome, not avoided.

The Tale of Time

Time has much to tell us if we listen. Table 2 shows us how time tells us what we value, how well we manage students within our classrooms, the quality of instruction we provide students, and the quality of students' learning. When we combine what time tells us with the results of research on time, we have identified important steps to improve the quality of education for all our students.

Table 2
Educational Meaning of Time

This Aspect of Time	Tells Us About
Allocated time	Our educational values (i.e., what we believe to be important for our children to learn).
The discrepancy between allocated and instructional time	The ability of teachers to manage their classrooms and their students.
The discrepancy between instructional time and time-on-task	The ability of teachers to provide high quality instruction to their students.
The discrepancy between time-on-task and academic learning time	The quality of student learning in our schools and classrooms.

References

Anderson, L. W., ed. *Time and School Learning*. London: Croom Helm, 1984.

Anderson, L. W.; Ryan, D. W.; and Shapiro, B. J., eds. *The IEA Classroom Environment Study*. Oxford: Pergamon Press, 1989.

Burns, R. B. "How Time Is Used in Elementary Schools." In *Time and School Learning*, edited by L. W. Anderson. London: Croom Helm, 1984.

Denham, C. H., and Lieberman, A. *Time To Learn*. Washington, D.C.: National Institute of Education, 1980.

Fisher, C. W., and Berliner, D. C., eds. *Perspectives on Instructional Time*. New York: Longman, 1985.

Fisher, C. W.; Filby, N. N.; Marliave, R. S.; Cahen, L. S.; Dishaw, M. M.; Moore, J. E.; and Berliner, D. C. *Teaching Behaviors, Academic Learning Time, and Student Achievement: Final Report of Phase III-B, Beginning Teacher Evaluation Study*. Technical Report V-1. San Francisco, Calif.: Far West Laboratory for Educational Research and Development, 1978. (ERIC ED 183 525.)

Frymier, J. "Learning Takes More Than Time on Task." *Educational Leadership* 38(1981):634–49.

Gage, N. L. *The Scientific Basis of the Art of Teaching*. New York: Teachers College Press, 1978.

Phillips, D. C. "The Uses and Abuses of Truisms." In *Perspectives on Instructional Time*, edited by C. W. Fisher and D. C. Berliner. New York: Longman, 1985.

Smyth, W. J. "A Context for the Study of Time and Instruction." In *Perspectives on Instructional Time,* edited by C. W. Fisher and D. C. Berliner. New York: Longman, 1985.

Stallings, J. "Allocated Academic Learning Time Revisited, or Beyond Time on Task." *Educational Researcher* 11(1980):11–16.

Stodolsky, S. S. *The Subject Matters.* Chicago: University of Chicago Press, 1988.

Chapter 4

Changing the Cosmology of the School Schedule

Fenwick W. English

A cosmology is an explanation of the origin of the universe and how humans fit into it, as well as the interrelationships of space and time (Runes, 1984). In ancient times, it consisted of myths that linked legends, demons, and dragons together to create an understandable universe (Campbell, 1973). Such myths are still important to humans. In fact, humans still live by them and their respective cosmologies.

When certain cosmologies become interlocked and assume a temporal dimension (space and time), a form is produced that becomes recognizable. A school is an architectural frame combining several cosmologies, notably a view of time as linear and divisible, and the idea of separating the knower from the known. The former was advanced by Aristotle, the latter by Descartes.

Schools, Clocks, and God

Current school cosmologies embrace a triparte notion of time as linear and capable of being compartmentalized into three dimensions—past, present, and future. A human being can exist apart from each of these three spaces. The separation of the knower from the known is thus possible. This separation was epitomized by Rene Descartes in his famous epigram, "I think, therefore I am." This Cartesian concept implied that one could think about oneself "outside of" oneself. One could create separate entities such as truth/fiction, body/mind, and objectivity/subjectivity.

School schedules are firmly rooted in Aristotelian notions of the separation of time, and Cartesian dualities. The clock is a significant expression of Aristotelian and Cartesian thinking. The clock's linearity expressed in hourly ordination translates into the western view of time as "monochromatic." In the West, one learns to do "one thing at a time," which leads to the important cultural value of "being on time." Eastern cultures, on the other hand, are polychromatic; they permit one to do many things all at once. Hence, one is not "late" when one is not "on time" (see Hall, 1969, pp. 173–74).

The western Christian church quickly embraced clocks and moved them inside the religious buildings to remind worshippers that God was the master clock maker who set the world into motion. God was timeless and perfect. Eastern churches, on the other hand, refused to allow clocks in their places of worship (Hightower, 1990).

When the industrial revolution arrived, with its factories run by bells and whistles with clock shifts, overtime, and time and motion studies, the rise of western technology was already linked to the dominant religious cosmology and rooted in the ancient Greek world. The school schedule is the operational manifestation in a secular institution of a peculiar form of "cultural imperialism" (Hall, 1977).

The principal develops a schedule and sets it into motion. The schedule then runs the entire school and all the teachers and students, much like medieval notion of God and his relationship to the world. In the late eighteenth century, modern concepts of schooling that emerged in Europe were tightly linked with traditional cosmologies. Schools, along with prisons, armies, and health providers, became the agencies that exercised social control in our society.

According to Foucault (1977), four main disciplinary techniques emerged in the school in the late eighteenth century. They were:

> the division and distribution of bodies in space, the division of time—and therefore activity into periods, the detailed control of activity, and the creation of tactical networks for the efficient deployment of bodies and activities (Jones, 1990, p.80).

A school schedule may be considered a temporal "tactical network" creating social discipline in a school. Unfortunately, traditional schedules are firmly grounded in cosmologies that have come under severe attack in modern times.

No Place for Humans in a Perfect World

The classic problem with viewing the universe and the world as part of a perfect clock is that there is no place for human will or choice. In philosophy, this dilemma has been called "Hume's problem." David Hume, when confronted with this dilemma, became skeptical of the idea that repeated human experiences could predict the unknown future. The assumption here is one of continual repetitions (like a clock perpetually ticking). Hume concluded that there was no reasonable basis for predicting the future based on the past. In that instant, Hume became an "irrationalist" (see Popper, 1979, p.4).

The cosmology of the school schedule assumes a perfect mechanical cycle that leaves out human will, any experience that is unique, and all that is known about how humans learn. It epitomizes the school as a dull, repetitive, lifeless place, devoid of any purposive inquiry. As mentioned earlier, it also views the school as an agency of social control. It links factory to school as near mirror images; the concepts of one are reflected in the other. Consider such pairs as classroom-job shop, tracking and homogeneous groups-dedicated production line, mainstreaming-mixed model assembly line, school schedule-batch processing (see English, 1992, p.39).

The Battle for the Principalship: Clocksetter or Leader

These attendant cosmologies have pushed the principalship from one completely rooted in teaching and instruction to one where the principal rarely does any teaching (see Figure 2). The major duty of the secondary principal remains to develop and implement the school schedule. Regrettably, scheduling is a mechanical task that moves the principal away from the arts of teaching and instruction, and toward the arena of management. The further the principal is removed from day-to-day classroom teaching, the more the role is tied to "meta-management"; that is, to those tasks that govern the processes of teaching, rather than direct work with teaching and teachers (see Kuhn and Beam, 1982, p.326).

Current calls to return the principal to more "hands on" work with faculty and curriculum are not guaranteed even under site-based management, at least until the principalship is separated from the existing cosmologies of schooling.

Developing New Cosmologies that Support New Schedules

Contemporary philosophy long ago discarded Descartes. Yet, in the words of Hightower (1990), "Whatever lip service we pay to other ideas, and however certain we are of its Cartesian falsity, after three centuries we still behave as if we lived in a Cartesian world" (p.158).

The work of Heidegger abolished the Aristotelian linearity of past, present, future, and established that there is only presence. The past is always a reconstruction of the present. And the future is only a presence extended from the present, not a clearly delineated separate state from the one in which we live (Rapaport, 1989).

The dualities of the Cartesian world have been shattered, excluding clean distinctions between the objective and the subjective. Such categories are language-dependent constructs.

In the words of Hightower (1990) ". . .'objectified' science is a construction based on a belief system, so it too must be understood as an aspect of mythology" (p. 151). Moving away from a mechanical device like a school schedule that is based on several interlocking and outmoded cosmologies, then, cannot be construed as more or less "scientific."

Figure 2
Historical Development of the Principalship

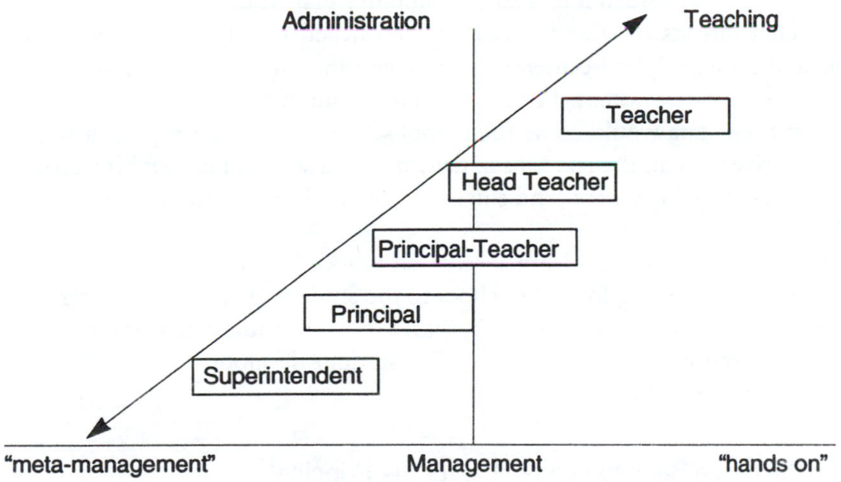

25

To construct an alternative to existing school schedules, one has to abandon the primary purpose of such devices: to control. Schedules control schools. They make schooling predictable. As we engage in conceptualizing alternatives, we must not fall into the trap of Cartesian dualities; i.e., to change from one form of control does not mean the school becomes out of control. What may happen is simply shifting control from an institutional anchor to teachers and students themselves. Moving from a six-period day to an "open block" schedule may involve some shifting of the control of teaching and learning from the institution to its clients. It is not just a matter of the form, although form is important. Rather, it is a matter of shifting the focus.

The schedule is a manifestation of the social control at work in schools. That schedules vary in length and frequency of time during a week is not the point. Changes in schedules will be nothing more than cosmetic until the teacher/student relationship is made the hub of a new cosmology for the school—a supporting web instead of chains that bind.

A Learner-Centered School Schedule

School schedules have been computerized since Dwight Allen's early work at Stanford University in the '60s. Allen sought schedules that permitted and encouraged modes of instruction beyond the self-contained classroom. Large group, small group, tutorial, and independent study were part of the new school schedule. Yet, despite such differentiations, once the schedule was set into place, it ceased to be "flexible."

A shift in cosmologies might mean that each student would carry his or her own computer and develop a personalized schedule to fit his or her individual interests and the recommendations of teachers. Ownership of the schedule would depend on the student acquiring the means to carry it out—a computer.

Imagine each student with a personal laptop computer punching in courses, desired times, types of instruction, length of study, and teachers. These selections could then be downloaded into a larger computer that would develop common possibilities. Such threads or strands would be reconciled by all possible means within a school, and a kind of pupil-centered learning continuum would be created that would maximize the greatest potential of the possible commonalities.

From these data would come the school schedule. Such an approach was used in more primitive form in the late '60s in daily demand scheduling. Sophisticated continuous progress schedules were (and still are) created. The technology is the least of the problems.

At the heart of the new learner-centered school is a fundamental transfer of the responsibility for learning from the school to the student. Traditional master schedules are unnecessary. Rather, schedules are based on individual need, interest, learning style, and desired curricular experience. The student develops for himself or herself a personalized school schedule.

Tipping the Scale Back to Leadership for the Principal

At the same time, the principalship moves back to its teaching roots and leaves meta-management for a more "hands-on" posture toward teaching and learning. As a consequence, the principal is not in control of the school. Instead, the school controls itself as a learning place, and becomes a collection of "mini-schools" or common strands programmed by students based on their needs and the demands of the learning communities. These learning communities are composed of "four to seven teachers in the elementary or middle school level and eight to twelve faculty members at the high school level" (Hill, 1992, p.116).

Whatever form these student-programmed schedules take, they assume a principal as leader rather than manager, and envision the students in control of learning. We cannot stop the historic slide of the principal from teacher to manager (see Figure 2) until learners are repositioned from passive recipients poured into the schedule's mold to active partners and shapers of their own learning. Such a school would become an embodiment of Keefe's (1989) concept of a "personalized education" for each student, and Giroux' (1988) call for emancipation of students within a tradition of critical pedagogy.

Curricular Subjects and Knowledge

School schedules inevitably form around the prevailing concepts of curriculum. Traditionally, they centered on the historic disciplines of mathematics, history, language, geography, and science. Such disciplines are deeply embedded in the existing power relationships with their supporting cosmologies. These prevailing curricula, the control of time and space and conduct, the rules and sequencing of activities, all hearken back to monastic life in the middle ages where "silence" was the norm for proper study.

A monastic view of school, curriculum, and schedules is still dominant in nearly all western nations. To question the validity of the prevailing curricular disciplines along with their form and interrelationships to existing roles and architecture is to shake the very foundations of education as we have come to know and perpetuate them.

Many schedules that incorporate different forms of curriculum are simply variations of the dominant monastic view. Revolutionary schedules that shift control to the learner will not be dominated by specific curricular forms. Instead, as emancipatory devices, they will insist that the form follow the function, placing the learner in a personalized schedule.

What Kinds of Prerequisites in a Unique Schedule?

What raw data would learners require in order to develop personalized schedules? They would need to have some idea of the curricular offerings, and the possibilities of amending them in some form. For example, a student who wished to study a community theme of "inequality" would arrange subjects a different way than one who decided to pursue "communications." Chunks of curricular disciplines might be needed, instead of the whole discipline. Hybrid disciplines such as biophysics might be substituted for a course in biology and one in physics.

The boundary of the school would be expanded to include other institutions and organizations such as social welfare agencies, governmental offices, and hospitals. Traditional notions of the school would be expanded to include community agencies, libraries, and museums, which would be more tightly linked to the school in a personalized curriculum and schedule than the conventional "field trip" entails.

The boundary of inquiry could be expanded to include forms of technology, supercomputers, and satellite learning uplinked and downlinked into all parts of the world. These connections and extensions would be tied together by a learner-designed and connected schedule that would include what traditionally has been called homework. The new homework would be independent and guided practice, or exploration of an expanded curriculum—wherever it might happen to be physically located.

The New School Schedule

In this expanded vision of schooling, scheduled time is neither linear nor sequential as we have come to understand it, nor even just school-based. Rather, it is multi-faceted and simultaneous in scope.

The new school schedule will not be exclusively confined to a school, nor a schedule as it is commonly understood (i.e., a linear sequence of classes pursued within distinctive curricular disciplines within an architectural time and space—a sealed cell). As such, the new school schedule will not only emancipate students and teachers, but also enable the principal to re-establish himself or herself as a leader of teachers. Principals should think about redesigning school schedules not only to transform learning and teaching, but also to transform themselves as leaders.

Leadership is the art of empowering rather than controlling. Leadership is emancipatory. It is time to shift the cosmology of the school schedule to the present. It is time to cast the Cartesian dualities and gridlock of the past into the junk heap. It is time to remake Aristotelian time so that a different and more liberating future can be constructed.

References

Campbell, J. *The Hero with a Thousand Faces*. Princeton, N.J.: Princeton University Press, 1973.

English, F. W. *Educational Administration: The Human Science*. New York: Harper Collins, 1992.

Foucault, M. *Discipline and Punish*. London: Allen Lane, 1977.

Giroux, H. A. *Schooling and the Struggle for Public Life*. Minneapolis, Minn.: University of Minnesota Press, 1988.

Hall, E.T. *Beyond Culture*. Garden City, N.Y.: Anchor, 1977.

————. *The Hidden Dimension*. Garden City, N.Y.: Anchor, 1969.

Hightower, J. *Myth and Sexuality*. New York: New American Library, 1990.

Hill, J. C. *The New American School*. Lancaster, Pa.: Technomic, 1992.

Jones, R. "Educational Practices and Scientific Knowledge: A Genealogical Reinterpretation of the Emergence of Physiology in Post-Revolutionary France." In *Foucault and Education,* edited by S. J. Ball. London: Routledge, 1990.

Keefe, J. W. "Personalized Education." In *Organizing for Learning: Toward the 21st Century,* edited by H. J. Walberg and J. J. Lane. Reston, Va.: NASSP, 1989.

Kuhn, A., and Beam, R. D. *The Logic of Organization*. San Francisco: Jossey-Bass, 1982.

Popper, K. R. *Objective Knowledge*. Oxford: Clarendon Press, 1979.

Rapaport, H. *Heidegger & Derrida: Reflections on Time and Language*. Lincoln, Nebr.: University of Nebraska Press, 1989.

Runes, D. D. *Dictionary of Philosophy*. Totowa, N.J.: Rowman and Allanheld, 1984.

Year-Round Education: It's Time

Chapter 5

Charles Ballinger

Year-round education is a timely idea. It holds promise for all American schools because it reshapes conventional thinking about the school year: when to start, when to end, when to take vacations, and whether or not to lengthen it. When new thinking about the school year emerges, older ideas about school organization are challenged and ultimately disappear.

It is increasingly difficult for educators to defend the September-to-June calendar, a calendar that was organized for the needs of a largely agricultural nation, when extra hands were needed during the peak growing season. It has served the needs of the nation well, but its time has passed.

Furthermore, this calendar is not an educational calendar; it never was. It is time to reconsider whether a calendar based solely on the growing season sufficiently meets our educational needs. All states currently require fewer than half of the total days each year for instruction. Stated differently, most American children annually spend more days out of school than in school. Obviously, there is much room for rethinking and reshaping the school year.

Year-round education has two salient features: the school year is reorganized to provide more continuous learning, and the long summer vacation (which year-round educators call the long summer of forgetting) is reduced.

Reorganizing the instructional year is a relatively easy task on paper. The administrator and staff willing to take the risk of challenging tradition develop a different pattern of student attendance. Two common patterns exist: Sixty days in school (12 weeks), followed by 20 days of vacation (4 weeks), repeated three times to obtain 180 days of instruction (referred to as 60–20); and 45 days in school (9 weeks), followed by 15 days of vacation (3 weeks), repeated four times yearly, to equal the usual 180 days (referred to as 45–15). Other calendars include the 90–30, 60–15, 30–10, 25–5, Concept 6, modified Concept 6, Personalized All-Year Plan, and a variety of others. Most are variations of—and are based on—quarter, trimester, or semester plans.

Regardless of names, all adjust to fit local circumstances; all provide periodic vacations; and all observe legal holidays. All reconceptualize in-school time; all consider out-of-school time to be as important as in-school time; and all seek to reduce summer learning loss.

Reducing Learning Loss, Frustration, and Failure

A study of school calendars conducted in 1978 for the Board of Regents of New York by George I. Thomas and several colleagues confirmed what teachers have known for decades: the reality of summer learning loss. This important and far-reaching study corroborated the practice of traditional teachers, who for decades have spent four to six weeks each autumn reviewing material from the previous school year that has been forgotten by students during the summer.

By rearranging the summer vacation into shorter periods of time, educators endorsing the year-round concept work actively to reduce summer learning loss, and to correct other longstanding problems of the traditional school calendar. In the lexicon of year-round education, the shorter, but more frequent, vacations are called "intersessions." By utilizing intersessions to the fullest, educators can begin to remediate or enrich student experiences. The contrast with a traditional calendar is startling.

In a traditional calendar, student frustration and fear of failure begin to build at the first instance of academic trouble, often soon after the school year begins. Unfortunately, most classrooms are not organized to deal with an individual student's instructional needs.

After nine unrelenting months, the failing student is encouraged to enroll in summer school to begin the process over again, often in exactly the same fashion and in the same sequence. How many adults, making their own decisions, would sit through nine months of failure and frustration and then willingly go through the same sequence again? Not many; but that is exactly what many students must do.

In contrast to the traditional scenario, a year-round calendar allows periodic breaks when more immediate and more rational intervention can occur. On a 45-15 schedule, for example, the scheduled three week break allows professional staff to mount an immediate remedial program to unblock problem areas for students. When a new nine-week instructional period begins, the struggling student is in a much better position to join with peers.

The intersession is not just remedial. It can also be rich in programs in the arts, computer science, nature, and a long list of other possibilities. Indeed, enrichment is often the best remediation for all students.

Year-round education, with its better-paced delivery of instruction, has other positive features. For example, those students who learn best by repetition are helped by continuous instruction and shorter vacation periods. Students who come from homes where the primary language is not English are a shorter time away from the language of the classroom.

Students on a year-round schedule come to realize that learning, like the work of adults, is continuous. Vacations come to be cherished as periods of refreshment rather than breaks that happen automatically. Shorter but more frequent vacations tend to be of greater variety, which in itself is educational. Families can experience leisure activities in all seasons of the year, avoid the summer hordes at national park and recreational areas, visit the best art shows and symphonic programs in winter, and generally have experiences not otherwise readily available, often at off-season rates.

Year-Round Education in Secondary Schools

Secondary schools are adopting alternative school calendars in record numbers. In addition to more continuous instruction and reduced summer learning loss, year-round schools report reduced student absenteeism, vandalism, and discipline problems. The frequent vacations in a year-round program reduce tensions between students and the demands of school, as well as between students and students, adding to the stability of the academic environment.

Those wary of restructuring annual learning time in secondary schools often raise concerns about cocurricular activities, varsity sports, student jobs, and student vacations. All these concerns are important to public and school life. Nonetheless, experience to date shows that altering the secondary school calendar has not damaged student activities, nor should it.

Students who want to participate in activities do so in a reorganized calendar school, just as they do in a traditional school. For several decades, young men have given up personal vacation in August to begin conditioning for football, while those choosing basketball forfeit time throughout the Christmas holiday period. Why wouldn't students agree to commit similar personal time on a year-round schedule? Educators who fear the worst for student activities have simply forgotten the drive exhibited by teenagers to do what they want to do.

Jobs for teenagers are by nature part-time and transitory. Usually the jobs are not affected by altering the school calendar.

Older high school students seeking employment come to realize that jobs are actually more plentiful when fewer students are seeking the openings at any one time. Graduating seniors can break into the labor market at varied times throughout the year. (High school students competing for summer jobs with college students are often the losers in the competition.)

Student vacations are less of an issue than most educators think. Time away from schooling has value. But how long must a vacation be to restore someone? Certainly not 10 to 12 weeks!

Most American families cannot afford, and do not take, extended vacations. One week, possibly two, out of town is the norm. Current news reports tell of other changing family vacation patterns: long weekends of three to four days are now common.

Benefits of Year-Round Education

Academic data on existing year-round secondary schools are promising. A number report higher achievement test results after implementation; others report significant gains in categorical programs. Most report fewer disciplinary problems; some report higher student and teacher attendance rates. While the trends are promising, proof waits for additional studies.

In addition to the educational benefits of changing the school year, there are social, economic, and political benefits as well.

Many persons—both in and outside the school community—believe that year-round education has potential to help curb social problems. For example, there is increasing uneasiness about having young people largely unoccupied, unsupervised, and unemployed for up to three months at a time. Our culture has allowed an explosive situation to develop. It is time, these youth advocates hold, to reduce the long, troubling summer by reorganizing the school year.

Economically, national voices are calling for all public agencies, including the public schools, to live within existing resources and to better utilize the financial support available. Specifically, these voices are calling for better use of existing school property and a longer school year.

Many educators bristle when economists, elected officials, and taxpayers say that school people must learn to live within existing resources. The typical rejoinder from educators is to call for more money. Although it is true that schools could do more for children if more money were available, it is also true that educators do not always use existing resources to the best advantage.

The National Governors' Association said it very well in its 1986 report, *Time for Results:*

> It makes no sense to keep closed half a year the school buildings in which America has invested a quarter of trillion dollars while we are undereducated and overcrowded (p. 3).

Most American school facilities sit idle for long stretches of time. Idle classrooms have neither educational nor economic value.

To capitalize on existing resources, about half of all year-round schools employ a technique called multiple tracking (or staggered scheduling) to allow enrollment of greater numbers of students in school buildings designed for lower enrollment. Costly new buildings are not needed to house additional students. Thus, scarce tax money is not further tied to brick and mortar.

In the battle for the tax dollar, curricular programs and staff salaries often go underfunded because too great a percentage of the available money goes to new buildings. Multiple track scheduling recognizes that savings of scale can be accomplished by allocating costs, including fixed costs, over a larger number of students.

Other voices in the economic and financial communities are calling for a longer school year, increased by 30 or more days a year. This form of year-round education allows more time for students to prepare for our nation's increasingly technological society.

Extending the year appreciably will cost more for additional salaries, utilities, and instructional supplies. At the current cost of $1 billion daily for the nation's K–12 public education, this may not be realized easily. But the change will come eventually, and now is the time to plan for it. All schools can begin to reorganize the school year.

Creative examples of reorganized and lengthened school years are available and can serve as models for schools to follow. More than 1,600 schools, including 300 secondary schools, have already abandoned the traditional school calendar.

The political force behind year-round education springs from the need for elected officers at all levels of government to show the public that students are doing "better," and that these more positive results are being achieved with the efficient use of existing resources. Year-round education has already demonstrated positive results in doing better, and it clearly has the edge over the traditional calendar in the efficient use of existing resources.

A Useful Question

The United States can no longer afford a school calendar that has outlived its usefulness. It is time to change. It is past time to rethink the traditional school calendar, and educators must take the lead.

It is useful to ask this question: Suppose that year-round education were the traditional school calendar, and had been for more than 100 years. If someone were to suggest a new school calendar that would exempt students from formal instruction for up to three months at a time, would the American public allow, or even consider, such a scheme?

The answer, of course, is no. Quite clearly, year-round education is a concept whose time has come.

References

Ballinger, C. E.; Kirschenbaum, N.; and Poimbeauf, R. P. *The Year-Round School: Where Learning Never Stops.* Bloomington, Ind.: Phi Delta Kappa Educational Foundation, 1987.

Glines, D. *A Primer on Year-Round Education.* Sacramento, Calif.: Association of California School Administrators, 1988.

National Governor's Association. *Time for Results.* Washington, D.C.: NGA, 1986.

Thomas, G. I., et al. *Learning, Retention and Forgetting.* Technical Report No. 5 of a Study of School Calendars. Albany, N.Y.: State Education Department, 1978.

Chapter 6

The Use of Out-of-School Time

Laurence Steinberg

Policymakers, researchers, and educational practitioners have usually focused their suggestions for school reform on influences on student achievement that occur within the boundaries of the school. Indeed, it would not be difficult to come away from the school reform literature with the impression that what adolescents learn depends entirely on what takes place within classroom walls.

How youngsters spend their time in school is certainly important, as many of the other contributions to this volume attest. But young people know—if sometimes educational researchers and policymakers forget—that teenagers' time outside school has an important influence on their academic performance and engagement in the classroom.

Some out-of-school activities, such as studying, reading, or attending cultural activities, are widely presumed to directly boost academic achievement. Others, such as working at a part-time job, or participating in school-sponsored activities, are generally thought to indirectly facilitate student achievement by contributing to character development or stronger attachment to the school. Still others, such as television viewing or partying with friends, are thought to interfere with education by exposing adolescents to values that are in conflict with those stressed in school.

Although popular belief in these assertions is widespread, careful research has called them into question. Many of the out-of-school activities believed to be deleterious are in fact innocuous. And some activities believed to benefit students are not advantageous at all; indeed, they may be harmful.

After-School Employment

The majority of American high school students—more than 80 percent—have school-year work experience prior to graduation. Approximately half of all sophomores, two-thirds of all juniors, and three-fourths of all seniors are in the labor force at some point during the academic year. Moreover, the time commitment of students to their jobs is substantial: the average working high school senior commits about 20 hours per week. Indeed, many high school juniors and seniors spend more time at work than in school.

Work experience proponents hope that time on the job will reinforce skills acquired in school. Unfortunately, studies of how adolescents actually spend their time on the job indicate that opportunities to use school-taught skills are quite rare. The typical adolescent spends almost no job time in activities involving reading, writing, or performing calculations—three job tasks that might enhance school performance.

Food service workers, for example, who constitute the most sizeable proportion of student employees, spend less than 2 percent of their work time using school-taught skills—only about one minute in every hour. Most adolescent work is dull, dreary, menial, and monotonous. Little of it is directly relevant to what students learn in school or what they will need for their adult jobs.

In view of the nature of the work performed by student employees, it comes as little surprise that after-school employment does little to enhance school performance. To the contrary, research consistently finds that school grades and school engagement are substantially lower among students who work long hours. Studies do indicate that disenchantment with school may impel students into part-time jobs, but longitudinal follow-ups over time find that working further exacerbates alienation. In other words, poor students are relatively more likely to work, but working long hours leads to their further disengagement from school. Moreover, the negative impact of work on school achievement is seen among college-bound students as well.

The amount of time students invest in jobs—not simply whether they work—emerges over and over as the key variable linking work with diminished achievement. In general, an important threshold in studies of student employment is about 20 hours per week, with the most substantial negative effect on school performance and engagement appearing among youngsters working more than this amount of time. Work in small doses—less than 10 hours weekly—does not seem to hurt school performance. Bear in mind, however, that nearly half of all high school seniors work in excess of 20 hours weekly.

There are a variety of explanations for why working long hours depresses school achievement. Perhaps the most obvious is that time at work displaces time that might otherwise be spent on school-related activities. Several researchers report that hours per week of employment is inversely related to hours spent on school activities; specifically, that students employed more than 20 hours per week spend less time on homework than their peers.

Very few American students—workers and nonworkers alike—spend much time on homework at all, however. (In our own studies of high school students, the average amount of time devoted to homework is less than five hours weekly.) It stands to reason, then, that the disengagement from school associated with extensive employment must be attributable to something other than, or in addition to, time on the job.

My colleagues and I have argued that extensive involvement in jobs actually undermines students' emotional investment in school. For example, students who work a great deal are absent from school more often, are less involved in school-sponsored activities, and report enjoying school less than their peers. One investigation showed that working students select less challenging courses. Several studies have found that student workers often employ questionable strategies to cope with school demands, including cutting classes, cheating, copying other students' homework, and lying about turning in required assignments.

Unfortunately, the impact of working on student achievement is not limited to individual students. We have reason to believe that having a large number of working students within a school changes the overall teaching and learning atmosphere, and that the effects spill over to nonworkers. Widespread student employment lowers teachers' expectations for their students, leading to less assigned homework and the increased use of class time for what would otherwise be out-of-school assignments.

Teachers are forced to adapt expectations and standards for students who are overly committed to working and who do not have the time, energy, or motivation to complete homework assignments.

Cocurricular Participation

Time spent in after-school activities explicitly endorsed by the school tends to increase school engagement. School-sponsored cocurricular activities are designed to strengthen youngsters' ties to schools, either by helping them make an emotional commitment to the institution or by creating close ties between students and the teachers who serve as coaches or club advisers. Such bonding can have impact on the academic domain.

On the other hand, commitment to any after-school activity takes time—time that might be directly invested in academic activities. Athletes, for example, especially those in the most visible sports, devote considerable time during the playing season to practice, training, and games. The time demands and performance pressures associated with some activities may leave participants too preoccupied or too fatigued to concentrate on schoolwork.

Excellence in a cocurricular activity, while desirable in its own right, may have the unintended effect of reducing necessary time spent on academics. This is especially likely in schools that lavish attention on exceptional athletes and other high achievers outside the classroom.

Initial studies of cocurricular participation and its impact on school performance did not yield consistent or clearly interpretable findings. In general, researchers found that students who participated in school-sponsored activities earned higher grades than their peers, but most of this research did not separate cause from effect. Some studies found that students involved in activities were more highly motivated to begin with, and that this motivational edge may have provided advantages in the classroom as well as on the playing field. Indeed, once motivational differences were taken into account, most of the "effects" of participation disappeared.

An important exception to this pattern exists. Studies indicate that although cocurricular participation may have a negligible impact on the achievement of average or above-average students, it may actually enhance the achievement of below-average students. One reasonable interpretation of this is that successful participation in school-sponsored activities does in fact help bond students—particularly those who might otherwise disengage—to the school.

Several points may be made about research on student activities:

First, our own research on time spent in student activities indicates that earlier studies probably took an overly simplistic view of the cocurriculum. We have found that the effects of participation on achievement vary with the number of hours invested, the specific type of activity engaged in, and the extent to which the activity diverts students from schoolwork. Students' grades go down when their time commitment to activities exceeds 20 hours weekly. (Unlike time spent on after-school work, few students clock this much time on cocurriculars.) Below this 20-hour threshold, student achievement increases with increasing hours of participation.

Second, the impact on achievement of participating in major sports (such as football and basketball) is negligible or sometimes negative, whereas the impact of participating in service, academic, and leadership activities (e.g., student government, newspaper, language clubs) is clearly positive. Participation in minor sports (wrestling, gymnastics, tennis) and in the performing arts falls somewhere between the two extremes.

Finally, and predictably, student performance suffers when the activity in which the student participates directly interferes with school-related responsibilities, and is enhanced when the activity fosters time-management skills. It would appear that participation in major sports leaves many students too drained of time and energy to devote sufficient concentration to their studies. Indeed, in some schools, student athletes are expected to practice both before and after school each weekday. Many of these athletes reported being nervous and distracted during class on the days of important games.

Our work also suggests that the values and attitudes of fellow participants matter a great deal. Students who devote a great deal of time to a particular activity spend much of their free time in the company of peers who share that interest. When these peers value academic accomplishment—more often the case in service and leadership activities than in major sports—this value is transmitted and reinforced through the informal contact with fellow participants. (Interestingly, we do not find that the attitudes of coaches or advisers matter very much.) As one student council member told us about her fellow council members, "They're pretty smart and they do pretty good in school. Yeah, it helps. 'Cause you want to get good grades like them."

Leisure

Along with time at work and in student activities, leisure constitutes yet a third out-of-school activity with potential ramifications for students' school performance and engagement. Studies of adolescent time use suggest that leisure—including socializing with friends—is the single most time-consuming activity of the average American adolescent.

Of course, leisure can mean many things. Adolescents are no more homogeneous in their tastes than adults. Just as one must differentiate among cocurricular activities in order to draw conclusions about their impact on student achievement, so one must differentiate among leisure pursuits to assess their effects on schooling. An adolescent who spends his free time programming computers with other "brains" will be affected in very different ways than someone who spends free time "kicking back" with the "druggie" crowd.

Considerable diversity exists within the adolescent population in leisure tastes and inclinations, but intellectual and academic pursuits are not common among today's teenagers. The majority of high school students spend less than 1 hour each week reading for pleasure, and one-fourth never read at all. Seventy percent devote less than 4 hours weekly to homework, while only 3 percent spend 10 hours or more on homework.

In contrast, the average American teenager spends approximately 20 hours each week watching television, 35 hours listening to music, and about 10 hours watching films or prerecorded video's. According to one review, even allowing for overlapping activities (e.g., reading while listening to music), the average adolescent spends roughly 8 hours daily with some form of mass media.

Research has shown the impact of leisure activities on school performance and engagement to be negligible. Most experts agree that pre-existing differences among adolescents in preferences and predilections probably drive teenagers toward some activities and away from others. Although time spent reading or on homework is associated with better school performance, a strong academic orientation probably leads students to read or study, rather than the other way around. Similarly, spending time watching television probably has little impact on adolescents' intellectual abilities, and rather reflects an interest in television.

Actually, the persons with whom students spend their free time may be more important than what they do with that time. This finding echoes research on the importance of peers in cocurricular activities. Indeed, peers exert a more powerful influence than parents on the school-related behaviors of high school students—behaviors such as time on homework, attending classes, completing school assignments, or concentrating during class.

The adolescent world is not characterized by a single, monolithic peer culture that is antagonistic to the values of adults; rather, it is composed of many different peer groups with quite different values and orientations toward school. Adolescents do select their friends in part because of similar values and interest, but friends exert an influence on each other above and beyond the initial similarity. All things being equal, a *B* student who spends time with friends who are *A* students stands a better chance of improving his or her grades than a *B* student with friends who are earning *C*s.

Conclusion

Taken together, research on students' time outside the classroom suggests four broad conclusions: First, students achieve more in school when the significant others around them value academic achievement—not only parents and teachers, but also their peers. Second, competing demands from nonschool activities may depress academic performance when these demands are time-consuming (more than 20 hours weekly) and do not relate to academic responsibilities (e.g., typical part-time employment). Third, academically marginal students are more susceptible to the effects—positive or negative—of out-of-school activities than are youngsters who are academically more secure. Schools should limit student time in nonacademic out-of-school activities to fewer that 20 hours weekly, if possible.

Fourth and most important, time spent in out-of-school pursuits is not in itself important simply because it displaces or reinforces school activities. How students spend out-of-school time affects their values and priorities, which in turn influences their behavior within the school. When students work long hours, they are likely to view school as their part-time job, something to be squeezed in during non-work hours. When they participate in school-sponsored cocurricular activities, however, their sense of belonging to school may be enhanced, and this may spill over into the academic domains. Regardless of the leisure activities in which they may be involved, students' attitudes and values toward school are profoundly influenced by the peers with whom they spend their out-of-school time.

References

Fine, G.; Mortimer, J.; and Roberts, D. "Leisure, Work, and the Mass Media." In *At the Threshold: The Developing Adolescent,* edited by S. Feldman and G. Elliott.

Cambridge: Harvard University Press, 1990.

Greenberger, E., and Steinberg, L. *When Teenagers Work: The Psychological and Social Costs of Adolescent Employment.* New York: Basic Books, 1986.

Steinberg, L.; Brown, B. B.; Cider, M.; Kaczmarek, N.; and Lazarro, C. *Noninstructional Influences on High School Achievement: A Research Review.* Madison, Wis.: University of Wisconsin-Madison, National Center on Effective Schools, 1988.

Chapter 7

Summary and Conclusions

Lorin W. Anderson and Herbert J. Walberg

None of the authors of this volume would equate time with learning, but all would agree that the wise allocation and productive use of time increases the chance that learning will occur and influences both the extent and quality of that learning.

Walberg (Chapter 1) states this point of view succinctly: "Increasing the amount of time available for learning and making [learning time] more productive are keys to improving learning."

The various authors offer suggestions for extending and enhancing learning time. These recommendations are summarized in Table 3, and are discussed briefly in this chapter.

Extending Learning Time

The most obvious strategy for the extension of learning time is to increase the school year. It is clear that American students spend fewer days in school each year than students in the majority of European and industrialized Asian countries. An extended school year can either be mandated by state or federal governments or achieved voluntarily through the intersessions of year-round education programs (Ballinger, Chapter 5).

Learning time can be extended by allocating sufficient time to those subjects and activities we believe to be the most valuable for our students and our culture. In this regard, Connelly and Clandinin (Chapter 2) argue that curriculum planning is, in essence, "organizing time."

Similarly, Anderson (Chapter 3) suggests that the way we allocate time informs us and others of our values. Is science less important than reading and language arts? The way we allocate time in elementary schools suggests this. Is memorization more important than critical thinking and problem solving? Time allocation in most secondary schools affirms this peculiar belief.

Learning time can also be increased by changing the ways schools and classrooms are managed. Schoolwide announcements and disruptions detract from available learning time. Similarly, poor classroom managers spend considerable time on procedural matters such as taking attendance, distributing materials, cleaning up, and disciplining students. Better management, both at the school and classroom level, almost always results in increased learning time.

Finally, learning time can be extended by helping students use out-of-school time more productively. Three very specific suggestions can be made in this regard (see

Steinberg, Chapter 6). First, students should be given more homework than is currently the practice. The fact that secondary school students, on a weekly basis, spend approximately 5 times as much time watching television as doing homework and almost 10 times as much time listening to music attests to the magnitude of this problem.

Second, after-school employment of secondary school students should be limited to no more than 20 hours per week. When employment exceeds 20 hours per week, students come to view school as their part-time work, and they spend insufficient time and effort on their schoolwork.

Third, every effort should be made to involve every student, particularly those with below-average academic performance, in cocurricular activities. These programs help students to develop the emotional ties with the school that are important to good time use and effective learning.

Table 3

Summary of Recommendations for
the Extension and Enhancement of Learning Time

Extending Learning Time

1. Increase the school year.

2. Allocate sufficient time to those subjects and activities believed to be most valuable for our students and our culture.

3. Change the ways in which schools and classrooms are managed.

4. Help students use out-of-school time more productively (e.g., increasing the quantity or quality of homework, engaging students in cocurricular activities that affirm the values of the school).

Enhancing Learning Time

1. Coordinate curriculum and instruction with the recurring school cycles.

2. Institute flexible scheduling to better meet students' interests and needs.

3. Increase students' emotional investment in their schools and the intensity with which they experience schooling.

4. Provide more continuous learning experiences for students.

5. Use instructional techniques and teaching strategies that involve students in learning and ensure their success in learning.

Enhancing Learning Time

After reading the chapters in this volume, it will come as no surprise to readers that there are many recommendations for the enhancement of learning time. Even Ballinger (Chapter 5) discusses the value of year-round education primarily in terms of enhancing learning time.

The following recommendations cut across the various chapters:

■ Coordinate curriculum and instruction with the recurring school cycles.

Holidays, athletic seasons, marking periods, class sessions, and lessons constitute cycles within which the teaching and learning process occurs. Enhancement of learning time depends to a large extent on the way in which these cycles are appropriately coordinated.

Steinberg (Chapter 6), for example, reports that student-athletes are nervous and distracted on game days. Clearly, learning is likely to be minimal under these conditions.

Similarly, Connelly and Clandinin (Chapter 2) describe the difficulty experienced by teachers whose classes must operate under arbitrary and fixed time periods.

■ Institute flexible scheduling in an effort to meet students' interest and needs.

"Learner-responsive" scheduling is more likely to result in enhanced learning time than scheduling based on administrative convenience and the need to control (English, Chapter 4). Technological advances (i.e., computers, videodiscs) make such schedules feasible to design and implement.

At least three basic questions must be answered before flexible scheduling can become a reality. Do we trust students to decide, in consultation with others, what are appropriate schedules?

Are we willing to expend the effort to "individualize" scheduling? Are we willing to tolerate some initial confusion in such scheduling?

■ Increase students' emotional investment in schools and the intensity with which they experience schooling.

Learning is not simply an academic matter. As Rothkopf (1976) has cogently pointed out, students have absolute veto power over their learning. Educators must find ways to decrease the likelihood that students will use that power. One of the best approaches is to get students "emotionally invested" in their schools.

This emotional investment may come from participation in cocurricular activities (Steinberg, Chapter 6). Similarly, developing schools and classrooms in which all students have a sense of belonging and regularly experience academic success is likely to produce the necessary "emotional investment" (Walberg, Chapter 1).

Students must understand that learning takes time and effort on their part, that it requires intensity. Simply stated, learning is students' work in school.

In Walberg's terms (Chapter 1), learning requires concentrated effort. We know that when students work more than 20 hours outside school, their intensity for schoolwork decreases.

Likewise, we should not be surprised that students (like most of us) enjoy avoiding work, choosing instead to spend their time socializing, watching television, or listening to music. Most of the chapter authors would agree with Connelly and Clandinin that we need to increase the "intensity by which time is experienced" by students.

■ Provide more continuous learning experiences for students.

In addition to more intense experiences, students need more continuous learning. For too many students, schooling is a set of discrete events rather than a continuous process. The connections between and among events are not clear to students (see English, Chapter 4).

Partly because of the concurrent cycles mentioned by Connelly and Clandinin in Chapter 2, students tend to think in terms of completing a project, a marking period, or their junior year, and then moving on to the next. Connections between projects, marking periods, and years are not clear. Connections among the various subjects are even more vague.

Walberg's observations (Chapter 1) about "spaced" and "massed" practice speak indirectly to the need for continuous student learning experiences. Only in a discrete world of clearly demarcated cycles could "cramming" for an examination be a viable option.

Ballinger (Chapter 5) is even more direct in his assertion about the success of year-round education in reducing forgetting, that students "come to realize that learning is continuous."

■ Use instructional techniques and teaching strategies that involve students in learning and ensure their success in learning.

In Chapter 3, Anderson points out that student success is the ultimate criterion for judging the effectiveness of learning time. There are at least two related aspects of this recommendation: First, the age-old tradition of teachers talking while students passively listen must be reconsidered. Questioning techniques, discussion groups, such peer work groups as cooperative learning, and the introduction of technology in schools and classrooms can increase student involvement.

Second, teachers must help students cultivate and use learning strategies that will enable them to succeed. Note-taking techniques, memorization training, and analytic and other strategies should be taught along with the traditional curriculum content to help students use their time more efficiently.

More than 40 years ago, Ralph Tyler (1949) wrote that learning depends on the activities and involvement of the learner. It is what the learner does that is learned, not what the teacher does. It is time that we acted on this knowledge.

A Closing Comment

Extending and enhancing learning time are likely to pay great benefits in terms of the quality of teaching and learning in our schools. We would be remiss, however, if we did not point out that most of the recommendations in this volume are not easy to implement. Many, in fact, require a different way of thinking about teaching and learning; in the current jargon, a paradigm shift.

Nonetheless, few educational variables have the potential that time does. Using time wisely and productively is a skill that we need for a lifetime.

References

Rothkopf, E. Z. "Writing To Teach and Reading To Learn: A Perspective on the Psychology of Written Instruction." In *The Psychology of Teaching Methods*, edited by N. L. Gage and D. C. Berliner. Chicago: University of Chicago Press, 1976.

Tyler, R. W. *Basic Principals of Curriculum and Instruction*. Chicago: University of Chicago Press, 1949.